Original title:
The Meaning of Life Is... Oh Wait, I Forgot

Copyright © 2025 Creative Arts Management OÜ
All rights reserved.

Author: Micah Sterling
ISBN HARDBACK: 978-1-80566-226-6
ISBN PAPERBACK: 978-1-80566-521-2

Metaphors of Not Quite Knowing

Like socks that disappear in the wash,
I ponder what I truly sought.
A cat that speaks in riddles,
While I'm lost in thought.

A spoon that stirs but never tastes,
A dance in mismatched shoes.
Life's a puzzle with missing pieces,
I change my mind like the news.

I used to chase down shooting stars,
Now I just chase my tail.
With every answer comes more questions,
In this never-ending tale.

Oh, look! A cloud shaped like a cat,
Is it wise or just absurd?
As I try to seek out reason,
I trip over each word.

When Clocks Stopped Ticking

Time stood still, like a frozen pie,
A moment caught in amber bliss.
I tried to count the seconds, though,
And ended up with this.

Each tick a joke I couldn't catch,
Each tock a moment gone.
I waved goodbye to minutes lost,
Then napped until the dawn.

When seconds turned to silly sounds,
Laughter filled the air.
I wore a hat made from my thoughts,
And danced without a care.

With clocks that looked like flying fish,
Who needs to know the time?
I spun around in dizzy joy,
It felt like a good rhyme.

Colors Fading at Dusk's Embrace

Crayons melting in the sun,
The reds, the blues all run away.
Am I the artist or the paint?
Oh, what a funny fray!

In evening's glow, I lost my hue,
My canvas only gray.
As night told tales of vibrant dreams,
I shrugged and chose to stay.

The sun's a wink, the sky a sigh,
Each tint a scattered thought.
When all the colors blend and fade,
What wisdom have I sought?

On this palette called the day,
I scribble with delight.
For fading's just a friendly wave,
In the soft embrace of night.

The Maze of Remembering and Forgetting

In a maze of thoughts, I wander lost,
A sign says 'This Way, Please'.
Turn left, turn right, and then I trip,
On memories like broken keys.

Each corner whispers tales of old,
But echoes lose their chime.
I search for paths that never were,
Guess I'll just run out of time.

Laughter hides behind the walls,
As I navigate this dream.
I found a door, but it was a wall,
Oh, how I want to scream!

Yet in this labyrinth of my mind,
I forge my silly route.
For forgetting's just a dance we do,
Where laughter's the best shout.

Moments Lost in Reflection

In the mirror, I ponder, a sight quite absurd,
A hair out of place, and oh, what's that word?
Life's daily circus, a playful parade,
I sip my coffee, and the thoughts start to fade.

A sock without a partner, they dance in despair,
The cat knocks a vase, as if he didn't care.
Chasing this wisdom, I trip on a thought,
Hoping the answers are not all for naught.

The Quest for Purpose at Twilight

Under the stars, I search for a clue,
In my pocket, some lint and a chewing gum too.
Lost in my quest for a grand kind of thrill,
I step on a twig and stumble downhill.

A squirrel gives advice, in a nutty refrain,
As I struggle to find the meaning of pain.
A shadowy figure beckons me near,
I ask for my purpose; he just sneezes, oh dear!

Fading Thoughts on a Painted Sky

The sun waves goodbye, the clouds start to blush,
I squint at the colors, oh what a rush!
A canvas of whimsy, it makes my heart sing,
Yet my grocery list feels like a daunting thing.

As day turns to night, my thoughts drift away,
I chuckle at memories that refuse to stay.
Like cotton candy dreams, they vanish with glee,
Escaping my grasp like a fish in the sea.

Enigmas of a Distant Horizon

A faraway land, where did it all go?
I once had a plan; it's now a big show.
With pies in the sky and a wink from the stars,
I scribble my hopes on imaginary cars.

Past the horizon, where secrets reside,
With gumdrops and laughter, I take a wild ride.
Gravity's light touch lifts me from the ground,
In this silly quest, joy is truly profound.

Sunsets That Fade Unnoticed

Colors blend as daylight dies,
While I ponder: where's my pie?
The sky's a canvas, bright and bold,
I chase sweet dreams, or so I'm told.

Forgot my keys, I turn around,
In the kitchen, lost and found.
These sunset views, they come and go,
But where's my snack? I need to know!

Countless Paths Left Untaken

I stand at forks, so full of glee,
Do I choose pizza or maybe tea?
Paths diverge, like thoughts in flight,
But first, a nap! That feels just right.

Dreams of grandeur fade away,
When faced with laundry, come what may.
Life's a maze without a map,
I bought new socks—time for a nap!

Whispers of Yesterday's Secrets

What was that plan I had in mind?
Oh right! Eat snacks, be unrefined.
Yesterday's wisdom slips my grasp,
Lost in giggles and a friendly gasp.

Forgotten lessons, tossed aside,
A slice of cake? I'll take a ride!
In the chaos, laughter swells,
With secret tales that no one tells.

Echoes from the Hollow Chambers

In the chambers of my silly brain,
Thoughts wander off like a runaway train.
Echoes linger, laughter and cheer,
Did I leave the stove on? Oh dear!

Life's a giggle, a playful jest,
Where's the map? I need to rest.
Hollow reminders call from the past,
But who needs wisdom when pie's a blast?

The Echoing Sound of a Closed Door

When I reach for keys, they vanish,
A mystery wrapped in my pocket.
Thoughts drift like leaves on the breeze,
Then I trip over my own shoelace.

I ponder great truths in my chair,
While my snack beckons with sweet whispers.
Did I leave my brain back at the store?
Ah, yes, checkout was a blur of doughnuts.

Conversations tread in circles,
Like my cat chasing its own tail.
Each answer hides behind a poker face,
As I blink, realizing I forgot.

Shimmers of Existence Beyond Recall

A dance among the stars, I ponder,
Yet my coffee's gone cold and bitter.
Chasing dreams on a paper boat,
While the cat judges from the window.

Time hiccups like a broken clock,
As I wonder what day of the week—
Is it Tuesday or just a feeling?
The calendar laughs, oh how cheeky!

Moments glimmer like fireflies,
Stars of memory fade like smoke.
Did I leave the stove on at home?
Nah, just another spark of forgetfulness.

Unfolding Pages of What Could Have Been

Each turn of the page feels foreign,
Books stacked high like my ambitions.
Maybe I'll write that bestseller,
Right after I find my pen again.

Conversations echo like bad jokes,
But laughter bursts like confetti.
Did I just agree to skydiving?
Oh wait, I'm scared of heights—and planes.

Plans drafted on napkins, crumpled,
Mistakes fixed with laughter and wine.
Where are my shoes—oh, they're on the roof?
My life's a comedy; hope you're laughing too.

Navigating the Labyrinth of Queries

Questions swirl like leaves in autumn,
Lost amidst thoughts and TV shows.
What's for dinner? I've forgotten,
Should I order pizza or just guess?

Maps of thoughts lead in circles,
Finding paths that are paved with snack bags.
Time to reflect on choices made,
But alas, where's the remote again?

Moments slip through like sand in hands,
Clocks tick loudly, mocking my pace.
Maybe wisdom lies in the fridge?
Or perhaps it's just last week's leftovers.

Chronicles of Intriguing Questions

Why's the sky so blue today?
Where did all my socks decay?
Is that a bird in a pickle jar?
Who knows why we parked so far?

Do aliens eat pizza in space?
What's the meaning of that strange face?
Did I leave the stove on again?
And what's this hair on my pen?

Can fish really swim upstream?
Where's my coffee? I need my cream!
Is my cat judging my snack choice?
Or does he just want a louder voice?

Life's a riddle, that much is clear,
Questions bubble like a cold beer.
Yet every time I think I know,
I trip on thoughts that go "Whoah!"

A Breath, Then Silence

I paused to ponder why we sneeze,
While dancing with a gusty breeze.
Is it good luck or just bad fate?
Did I forget to check the date?

Why do we cry during sad films?
Can pancakes fly on fluffy whims?
And when I laugh, does the world shake?
Does my toast burn for fun or sake?

Sometimes I wonder what's for dinner,
Will ice cream make me a winner?
Does sock puppetry hold my fate?
Or am I just thinking too straight?

So here I sit with a grin wide,
As thoughts and giggles collide!
More questions tumble, what a show,
Hold on tight, let's see where we go!

The Flicker of a Wandering Flame

A candle flickers unsure of its place,
Is it maintaining a steady grace?
Or planning to dance with the ants around?
What secrets does a flame confound?

Why do we count sheep at night?
Will they lead us to insight?
Or instead, give us wacky dreams?
Of ice cream mountains and chocolate streams?

What is a sock with no pair?
Just a loner without a care?
Do phones have feelings, too, I fear?
When they drop calls, are they sincere?

In this silly quest for clues,
Life's many riddles amuse.
For each answer brings giggles anew,
As questions twirl in a playful queue.

In the Wake of Overlooked Journeys

I packed my bags for great unknowns,
But left my keys on the kitchen's stones.
With socks on my feet, I hit the road,
Just me and my thoughts, oh, what a load.

I asked the GPS where to go,
It sent me to a taco stand, though.
Adventures await in the silliest places,
Filled with laughter and a few funny faces.

Lost my wallet, but made a friend,
Turns out, life loves to mix and blend.
So here's to messes, chaos and cheer,
Each turn of events brings us near.

Finding joy in each blunder and twist,
Life's a dance—don't put it on your list.
We'll giggle and grin, it keeps us alive,
Forgetting the map was the best way to thrive.

Unspoken Questions on Calming Waves

Waves whisper words, but I can't hear,
Are they asking for snacks, or just being clear?
While building sandcastles, my towel took flight,
Chasing the seagulls on a sunlit night.

Why do I trip on shells, oh so small?
Each tumble a lesson, or perhaps just a fall.
But the ocean's laughter drowns my plight,
Salt and sand make everything right.

With a bucket of crabs as my loyal crew,
I ponder if fish dream of skies so blue.
As I sip from a coconut, tasting the breeze,
I laugh at the sun and its playful tease.

So here I will sit, with questions galore,
Embracing the waves while they scatter ashore,
Maybe the answers can wait for a while,
For laughter and sun are always in style.

Revelations Found in Simple Things

A cup of coffee, the world's a stage,
Where dreams take flight, unbound by age.
With a dash of cream and a sprinkle of glee,
I ponder the universe, but not too seriously.

In the garden, I saw a snail take a stroll,
He moved so slow, but he reached his goal.
Each flower a giggle, each leaf a wink,
Nature's a joker, don't you think?

Belly laughs echo in every small space,
While chasing after socks that run from grace.
Simple joys wrapped in everyday stuff,
Like finding lost keys or an old, furry muff.

So let's toast to the quirks that life brings along,
With missteps and laughter, we can't go wrong.
Embrace the absurd, let life's whimsy sing,
For wisdom finds us in the simplest thing.

Chasing Fireflies Beneath the Stars

In the backyard, the night lights glow,
Fireflies flicker, putting on a show.
With jars in hand, we run and squeal,
Each little spark feels vividly real.

Moments captured like time stands still,
As we chase the magic, and laughter spills.
Under the moon, we weave silly tales,
Of pirates and dragons, of ships with sails.

But what of the stars, so high and so bright?
Do they giggle at us in the warm summer night?
With every wish whispered, or cake left to share,
Life's a wild ride, but oh, do we care!

As we catch our breath, in this whimsical game,
In the heart of the night, we all feel the same.
With fireflies dancing through darkness afar,
We find glimpses of wonder, like catching a star.

Shadows of What Once Was

Once I had a brilliant thought,
But then it ran away, I swear!
Chasing shadows of my past,
I trip over my rocking chair.

In the attic, dust bunnies hide,
They whisper secrets, oh so sweet.
I nod along, forgetting why,
Then reminisce on my last tweet.

Was it cheese or was it bread?
Or was it something quite absurd?
My memories are like quicksand,
They sink away, not a single word.

As laughter echoes through the halls,
I ponder life's quirks with a grin.
Tripping over cosmic calls,
Maybe next time, I'll take a spin.

Time's Elusive Hand

Tick-tock goes the clock, oh dear,
What was I doing, was it here?
In a race with time's sly grin,
I lose the plot, I never win.

Oh wait, did I say that aloud?
I meant to chuckle, not sound proud.
Time ticks past on silver wings,
While I ponder foolish things.

A moment flits, a wisp of breeze,
I wave goodbye with such unease.
While moments blend in perfect chaos,
I sit with snacks, oh what a boss!

The hourglass spills grains of joy,
Yet I remain a clueless boy.
With each tick, I'll dance once more,
And forget what I was searching for.

The Pause Between Breath and Thought

In the stillness, thoughts entwine,
One second's pause, oh how divine.
But just as clarity draws near,
My cat jumps up, jumps on my beer.

I chase distractions near and far,
Like counting clouds, or wishing on a star.
Each moment stretches, bends, and fades,
While I'm stuck in this puzzle maze.

Who knew a trip to the kitchen,
Would lead to pondering life's mission?
I grabbed a snack, forgot my plan,
Now I'm the snack-time guru man.

In the pause between breath and thought,
I find the joy that can't be bought.
With laughter and crumbs upon my lap,
I face the world, with my playful map.

Fragments of a Fleeting Truth

I scribble notes on napkin scraps,
Fragments lost within my naps.
What was the wisdom I once wrote?
Ah yes, it involved a weird goat.

Pies in the sky, what do they mean?
Meringue on clouds? That must be keen!
But just when I think I've cracked the code,
I spill my drink and lose the road.

Truths bounce like balls in a game,
I chase them down, but they feel lame.
What is funny, what is real?
I laugh at nonsense, what a deal!

So here I sit, with giggles bright,
In this nonsense, I find delight.
Fragments collected, a quilt of cheer,
In the chaos of life, I draw near.

Reflections in the Mist of Time

In a mirror, I glance, a face I don't know,
Searching for wisdom where bubbles might blow.
Tick-tock goes the clock, but I'm stuck in a swirl,
Did I leave my keys, or just lost in a whirl?

Sipping on coffee, with thoughts all a-jumble,
Recalling the moments of laughter and fumble.
Was it a dream, or did I really snore loud?
Guess I'll just wave to my past self — a crowd.

Dancing through memories, I trip on the floor,
Chasing lost thoughts like a dog with a score.
Wrapped in confusion, like candy on a stick,
At least if I fall, it's a comedy flick!

So here I stand, with a grin full of cheer,
My life's a good joke that I might never clear.
Mirthful reflections, with a wink and a jest,
Maybe forgetting isn't the worst, but the best!

Trials Written in Sand

Building my castles, with dreams at high tide,
Carving my hopes where the seagulls reside.
But as the waves crash, they wash them away,
Is my life just a game where the rules will not stay?

Each grain is a moment, a laugh or a frown,
A footstep, a stumble, then back to the town.
I wrote a grand novel, but the tide had its say,
That's what happens when you write by the bay!

With buckets and shovels, I dig for a clue,
Where is the wisdom? Is it lost like a shoe?
I'll find it someday, right after I nap,
For wisdom's a treasure, wrapped tight in a trap!

So here's to the trials that shift with the sea,
Each wave tells a story, so playful and free.
I laugh at my plight, with a twist of my fate,
Maybe life's silly — I'll just celebrate!

Hummingbird Wings and Missed Opportunities

Flying around like a thought on a string,
Sipping on nectar, oh, the joy that it brings.
But wait — did I leave the stove on again?
It's hard to remember when you're dancing with Zen!

A blink and I'm gone, just a flash in the sun,
Chasing my dreams, but they seem on the run.
Last week, I swore I'd finish that book,
Now here I am, in this kitchen I cook!

I'll catch that next chance, just you wait and see,
Like catching a whiff of fresh-baked pastry.
But wait, what's the recipe, please give me a sign,
Oh dear heavens — where did I put that line?

Yes, life flutters past like those wings in a blur,
Each moment a prize, but what was that slur?
With laughter in hand and my mind in a spin,
I'll toast to missed chances — let the games begin!

The Puzzle of What's Left Behind

Peering through boxes, what treasures are here?
A sock with a hole, a toy from last year.
Each fragment of memory, a puzzle in place,
But where's the corner piece, the one with my face?

Sorting my life like a jigsaw gone mad,
Finding old photos that make me feel glad.
Wait, did I wear those brightly striped pants?
It seems I was the king of awkward dance!

Threads of connection, they weave and they tangle,
My thoughts like spaghetti, they twist and they dangle.
Yet, laughter erupts as I stumble along,
Each piece tells a story, and some bits are wrong!

So here's to the remnants that clutter my mind,
Each shard of my history just waiting to find.
I'll cherish the chaos, it's part of my plan,
For life's just a puzzle — now where's that piece, man?

Laughter Amidst the Chaos

In midst of trials, we trip and fall,
With socks mismatched, we laugh through it all.
Spilled coffee brings giggles, oh what a sight,
Life's little blunders, pure comic delight.

Chasing forever, yet losing our way,
We dance in circles, come what may.
With hiccups and snickers, we find our groove,
In this wild ride, we've nothing to prove.

How many times did we lose our keys?
Or miss the bus sneezing, with each of our wheezes?
Life's riddles tickle, like feathers in flight,
We'll laugh through the chaos into the night.

So here's to confusion and ridiculous fun,
Let's toast to the mishaps, one by one.
For in this laughter, we're truly alive,
Fumbling through moments, we learn how to thrive.

Scattered Seeds of Wonder

Seeds of thought scattered, fresh in the breeze,
We plant them in laughter, like wildflower tease.
One grows into chaos, another takes flight,
Bizarre little mysteries spark joy and delight.

In gardens of muddle, we splash and we play,
With each silly moment, we brighten the day.
A frog on a lily, a bird in a hat,
Life's quirks remind us, 'Hey, how about that?'

Chasing our dreams with custard on face,
We paint our grand vision in a splashy embrace.
With giggles as soil, we cultivate cheer,
In the vastness of wonder, there's nothing to fear.

So toss out your worries, embrace the surreal,
Let whimsy be king, that's the ultimate deal.
For in scattered laughter, we're never alone,
Together we flourish, in chaos, we've grown.

Fleeting Glimpses of Forever

Through windows of whimsy, we sneak a quick peek,
At moments so silly, they leave us quite weak.
A cat on a skateboard, a dog with a kite,
Here's to the strange sights that give us delight.

Like bubbles that pop in the warm summer air,
We whirl through our days without a single care.
Winking at time, it can run, it can pause,
In fleeting delights, we find the real cause.

We dance with absurdity, misstep and twirl,
With giggles and chuckles, we give life a whirl.
For each fleeting moment, a treasure we keep,
In laughter's embrace, we find joy in the leap.

So let's gather our wonders, our quirks and our glee,
In this topsy-turvy world, join in the spree.
For as fleeting as life is, we wink and we jest,
And in every laugh, we find our true quest.

A Canvas of Forgotten Meanings

A blank canvas whispers, what shall we paint?
With splotches of laughter, and moments quaint.
A splash of the silly, a stroke of the odd,
In the art of existence, we all play the god.

Colors collide in a beautiful mess,
Each blunder a masterpiece, life's own caress.
A wig on a rabbit, a joke in the sky,
With each hearty chuckle, we learn how to fly.

The palette of time is both vivid and bright,
As we scribble our stories, oh what a sight!
A mural of moments, all mishaps embraced,
In the joy of the journey, the canvas is graced.

So pick up your brushes, let's make a grand splash,
In tailored confusion, we'll find our own stash.
For a canvas of laughter tells tales with great glee,
In the colorful chaos, we are truly free.

A Serenade to the Unseen

Balloons float past my head,
They whisper secrets, blue and red.
I chase them down with double scoops,
Yet forget my socks, surrounded by loops.

Elevators hum a silly tune,
While I ponder under the moon.
Where did I leave my coffee cup?
Did I really need all that stuff?

Dogs bark at squirrels, crazy sights,
Caught in their never-ending fights.
I laugh at clouds drifting away,
As I lose my thoughts in a ballet.

What is this game and where's my score?
Was there a plan? I can't ignore.
But life's a dance, an odd refrain,
I'll spin again, forget the gain.

Unraveling Threads of Cosmic Queries

A pencil rolls off my desk,
Where did it go? I can't contest.
Under the couch? Or in my shoe?
A grand adventure's overdue!

Stars flicker in the evening glow,
Why do best friends steal your nacho?
Cosmic questions fill the night,
Should I embrace the silly fright?

Maps that lead me on wild chases,
Have taken me to strange places.
Is that my lunch in yesterday's bag?
Oh dear, that does sound like a drag.

I ponder over meals gone cold,
And wonders, both shy and bold.
In laughter, I find the grand design,
Oh wait, what was that? Never mind!

Pieces of a Jigsaw Never Fitted

Gray skies shuffle with bright confetti,
Each thought I have feels unsteady.
Did I forget my keys again?
Or is it just a cosmic pen?

I try to fit the pieces right,
But none of them ever feel quite bright.
Like socks that fight a laundry war,
They're hiding in a distant drawer.

Coffee spills as I trip and slide,
Making sense of the chaos, wide.
The cat looks up as if to say,
"Life's a puzzle, just go play!"

I giggle as I chase my tail,
Wondering where I'll next set sail.
Life's antics spin around my head,
Oh look, more crumbs, and I'm still fed!

Dusty Roads with No Destination

Dusty roads stretch out afar,
Winding paths, a quirky bazaar.
I trip on dreams and laugh a lot,
In search of wisdom, I find a pot.

Signs point left, signs point right,
But where's the road to genuine light?
I wave at clouds and chase the breeze,
Yet forget the name of all my keys.

Sidewalks twist like gummy worms,
Engaging in their silly terms.
Laughter echoes in the air,
Turns out it's just an old teddy bear!

Each whim takes me in a spin,
With each lost thought, I dive back in.
Oh, where's that tape I meant to buy?
Oh wait, did I just lose my tie?

Chasing the Dust of Lost Moments

I chased my dreams with a cup of tea,
But all I caught was a bumblebee.
With every step, I slipped on time,
And wondered if life was just a rhyme.

A sock's missing, did it run away?
Or did it hide from laundry's sway?
I laughed as memories fuzzed like cream,
And pondered if life's just one big dream.

Is that my lunch or yesterday's fare?
Whatever it is, it's filled with flair!
I laughed out loud, I sighed in jest,
For lost moments are still the best.

Perhaps my purpose's in the crumbs,
Or in the giggles that sometimes hum.
So here I am, with a wink and a nod,
Chasing moments, oh so flawed!

Gratitude Amidst the Nebulous

In a foggy haze, I sit and smile,
Counting my blessings, though they're a mile.
A missing shoe? A quirky sock?
Each oddity rocks the ticking clock.

I tripped on thoughts, sprained my mind,
But in the mess, sweet gems I find.
The cat just yawned amid the dust,
Gazing lazily, it's a must!

I raised my glass to toast the moon,
But spilled the drink; my thoughts were strewn.
Yet gratitude fills my puzzled heart,
For every stumble is a work of art.

So here's to chaos, mischief, and fun,
Every little folly under the sun.
I'll dance with clouds in this whimsical play,
Grateful for life, come what may!

Echoes of What Was Almost Real

In dreams I fly, or so it seems,
Yet land in puddles of ice cream.
Half a thought, a whispered breeze,
How quickly life bends at its knees.

I thought of truths, then forgot the plot,
Frolicked with ghosts in a dreamy spot.
What was almost real? A shadow's sway!
Yet life's a joke in a funny way.

I wore my pants inside out today,
And strolled about in a merry display.
Do I worry? Nah, it's all absurd,
My heart sings loud, though words get blurred.

So here I hum with a wink and cheer,
For echoes ring true, and we're all here.
In laughter's embrace, we surely thrive,
What was almost real? Oh, I'm alive!

Restless Nights on the Path of Wonder

Under a blanket of dust and stars,
I tossed and turned with dreams of jars.
Were they filled with wishes? Oh, who could tell?
As thoughts spun around like a spinning carousel.

What was I searching for in the night?
A chocolate fountain? A dragon's flight?
My bed's a ship sailing storms untold,
Restless nights, oh, how bold!

I peered outside, seeking the moon,
Wishing for answers, perhaps too soon.
Each giggle echoed, a playful tease,
Life's a puzzle, but I love the breeze.

So I drift off, embracing the jest,
In dreams where the wildest thoughts rest.
For on this path, both silly and bright,
Restless nights give way to delight!

In Search of a vanishing Star

I sought a guide with sparkling eyes,
Hoping they'd show me the cosmic lies.
They giggled and slipped through my hands,
Leaving me pondering in strange lands.

I chased the glow of fading light,
Each twinkle a tease in the endless night.
But laughter echoed through the black,
As I tripped on dreams, never looking back.

I asked the moon for a silly jest,
But all it did was shine its best.
A comet whizzed by with a wink,
And I laughed so hard, I couldn't think.

Now I wander with a crooked smile,
Collecting moments, mile by mile.
In this treasure hunt that leads no where,
I find my joy in the cosmic air.

Unraveling Threads of Intention

In a closet of wishes, I found some yarn,
Tangled and frayed, but not meant to harm.
I pulled on a string, and it led to a sock,
That hopped away, tickling my clock.

I knitted a dream with laughter so bright,
But halfway through, it took flight.
A goose wore my sweater, it waddled about,
And I chased it down, but I had my doubts.

The fibers of fate got knotted in time,
Each pluck of the string unraveled a rhyme.
But the meaning escaped like a butterfly,
As I giggled, confused, oh my, oh my!

So now I crochet with glee in my lap,
Creating strange shapes, a whimsical map.
For in every loop, I find joy's embrace,
Tangled or not, I love this chase.

A Journey with No Map

With a sandwich in hand and shoes full of holes,
I set off to find where laughter unfolds.
But every turn led to sweets and a pie,
And I banished the thought of 'what's next' and 'why?'

My compass spun wildly, a dizzy delight,
Pointing at ice cream and dancing at night.
I questioned a squirrel about roads to my goal,
It shrugged, ate a nut, and rolled on a pole.

An old tree whispered secrets from days long past,
But all that I heard was the sound of a blast.
A party erupted, balloons all around,
As I joined in the fun, destiny unbound.

So here I am, without guidance or plan,
Laughing with friends, a whimsical clan.
For each silly moment, I choose to embrace,
Is a map that leads to a joyful place.

The Sigh of an Unanswered Question

Once I pondered with furrowed brow,
What was the answer, and how, oh how?
But the question giggled, twirled on a chair,
And whispered secrets that danced in the air.

I asked a frog resting by the blue pond,
It croaked of mysteries, both short and long.
With each ribbit, I laughed out loud,
As the meaning slumbered beneath a cloud.

Then came a cat with a curious grin,
It looked at me, said, "Where do we begin?"
In that small moment, I finally found,
Silence holds laughter, in joy we're unbound.

So now I reside in the smiles of friends,
Where questions are tangled, and laughter transcends.
For in every sigh, a giggle might bloom,
And the heart finds its meaning in playful rooms.

Hazy Visions of Tomorrow

I woke up this morning, thoughts in a spin,
Did I forget a meeting or a trip to begin?
Coffee spills on my shirt, a cat's in my way,
That was important, right? Feline play all day!

Plans scribbled on napkins, where did they go?
A treasure map leading, but leads to just slow.
What was that thought? Did it slip like a kite,
Soaring high with the clouds, then lost out of sight?

Time hops like a bunny, with an odd little bounce,
Tick-tock says the clock, yet I just can't pounce.
Dancing with time, I step on my toes,
Every giggle a memory, who even knows?

So here I am laughing, on this whimsical ride,
Chasing shadows of thoughts that begin to collide.
In this circus of life, full of jests yet to tell,
The punchline always slips, oh well, what the hell!

Chasing Whispers Through Time

A calendar whispers, 'You missed all the fun!'
Each date wears a costume, but where has it run?
Did I schedule that dinner? Or trip to the sea?
Ah yes, it's all vanished, like socks in a spree!

Ghosts of good intentions, hiding in bins,
I brought them some snacks, now they're just grins.
Time is a sneaky little magician, you see,
Turning plans into smoke, oh how it fools me!

With watchful anticipation, I hover and sway,
What was I doing? It's all gone astray.
Chasing after whispers like butterflies fly,
They flit from my grasp, as I wonder, oh why?

In this funny showdown between now and then,
I'm battling with moments like a jester in ken.
The laughter erupts from the chaos I find,
As I wave to my memories, they dance out of mind!

The Dance of Uncertainty

Life spins a disco, with sparkles and flair,
Each step is uncertain, do I dance or declare?
A misstep to the left, then right, what a whirl,
Is that my intention, or just a twirl?

Questions bounce like rubber balls in my head,
Each echo empty, runs like a thread.
Where's the plan? Oh wait, I should know,
But it's stuck in a limbo, a no-show for show!

So I step on the beat of a whimsical dream,
Shaking off worries that dance in the stream.
Just follow the rhythm, let laughter take flight,
Even if every move feels slightly contrite.

Here I am swirling, with smiles and a glaze,
Sliding through time in this whimsical maze.
With each jab of the wink, life giggles with glee,
While I twirl in this dance, quite joyously free!

The Puzzle of Elusive Moments

Pieces scattered around in a jigsaw of glee,
What fits where? I swear it's a mystery.
A corner I grasp, oh, it slips through my hands,
Lost in the shuffle of life's busy strands.

Each moment a riddle, wrapped up in delight,
I ponder the answers late into the night.
Was it lunch with a friend or a stroll by the bay?
Now it's just fog, as it fades into gray.

Searching for that piece that brings it all clear,
The map of my thoughts feels just like a deer.
Skittish and fleeting, will it ever stand still?
Chasing a shadow with each laugh and each thrill.

But oh, what a journey this puzzle provides,
With giggles and wonders as my only guides.
So I gather the pieces and dance with my fate,
As life plays the game, I giggle at fate!

How to Capture an Unfathomable Dream

I reached for a cloud, oh so fluffy,
But it slipped right through, isn't that guffy?
Chasing my thoughts, like a cat with a string,
I trip on my shoes—what a silly thing!

The ocean of wishes, so deep and so wide,
Swam with a fish, then I took a ride.
It quickly turned back, with a wink and a grin,
Said, "Not today, friend, where do I begin?"

I wrestled a thought, that turned into cheese,
Oh, how it smelled, left me weak in the knees.
The more I explored, the less I could see,
But laughter erupted, boosting my glee!

So here's to the dreamers, both wacky and wise,
Who chase after shadows, beneath the blue skies.
Life's just a puzzle, with pieces that shift,
And those who can giggle, have truly found gift!

Reflections in a Shattered Mirror

A laugh in the glass, what a sight to behold,
Reflections of me, and some stories retold.
With each little crack, a new personality,
But why do I look like a patchwork reality?

I wink at the shards, and they giggle right back,
Holding the secrets in their shiny, sharp crack.
Each piece plays a role, like a cast in a play,
But who's got the script? I seem to mislay!

Oh, how I ponder, as I tidy my hair,
Do I really exist, or just float in the air?
As I pose for the mirror, it chuckles and sighs,
Said, "We all get confused, but you're quite the surprise!"

So let's toast our reflections, both goofy and neat,
With laughter as glue, our lives are complete.
In the realm of the broken, we find our true shine,
And humor in chaos, makes everything fine!

Wandering Thoughts on a Wandering Path

I wandered on Tuesday, got lost on my way,
A squirrel stole my snack, what a bold foray!
With each twist and turn, my thoughts danced around,
Finding joy in the mishaps, I wore as my crown.

A signpost stood tall, but it made no sense,
It read 'Go left, but maybe not – do it hence!'
I chose to go right, found a puddle to splash,
How could such a choice be made with such dash?

In the maze of my mind, every corner's a game,
With whispers of wanderlust, never quite the same.
Then I tripped on my shoelace, quite a grand fall,
I laughed with the daisies, as they answered my call!

So here's to the strolls, both silly and sweet,
Where thoughts go amiss and adventures repeat.
The world is a playground, don't stick to one path,
For laughter's the compass, a guide to great math!

The Sound of a Silenced Heart

In a world of quiet, my heart took a break,
Thoughts drifted along like a soft, gentle flake.
With a thump and a pause, I sat down to see,
What echoes in silence? A small mystery!

I tried to compose a sweet melody,
But all I could hear was a sneeze, oh me!
I bobbed and I weaved, in a rhythm so weird,
The sound of my thoughts? A laughter appeared!

So, I clapped my two hands, to summon some cheer,
The silence just giggled—like it knew I was here.
With each little chuckle, my worries grew slim,
Even silence can dance, if you let your heart swim!

Thus, here's to our hearts, so quiet yet bright,
They hum in the shadows, a fluttering light.
Let laughter be music, the song of our days,
For the sound of a heart can echo in plays!

The Art of Forgetting Why

In a world where thoughts do play,
I ponder as I drift away.
With every step, I lose my way,
A merry dance, come what may.

I had a plan, oh what a sight,
But like a bird, I took to flight.
The details vanish, out of sight,
I laugh at shadows in the light.

A grocery list from days of yore,
Now just a list of things I swore.
The trail goes cold by the front door,
But humorous hiccups, I adore.

I seek the wisdom in this game,
Embrace the quirky, not the shame.
Forgetful fun is my claim to fame,
Life's a jest, not a solemn name.

Cerulean Skies and Fleeting Glances

Beneath the broad, cerulean dome,
I search for thoughts, but feel like foam.
With every laugh, I lose my tome,
Amidst the vibrant intersperse.

A glance at clouds, my mind just drifts,
Is it a prank or just a gift?
Through fleeting thoughts, my spirit lifts,
In humor's embrace, my mood persists.

I waved at stars, forgot their names,
Their shining lights never bring me fame.
Yet still I play these silly games,
In comical dances, I'm never tame.

With breezy winds, ridiculous cheer,
I grasp for dreams that disappear.
While skies above hold secrets dear,
I chuckle at how nothing's clear.

An Ode to the Unremembered

Oh unremembered, dear old friend,
You've slipped away, but I pretend.
In laughter's heart, I must defend,
Your fleeting charm, on which I depend.

Thoughts come and go like passing trains,
What was I doing? See the remains.
A life of giggles and strange refrains,
With loose connections and funny chains.

I raise a glass to carefree glee,
To memories lost in a whispering spree.
Who needs the past? Just let it be,
With joy in forgetting, I'm truly free.

Let's toast to moments, both bright and dim,
To all the jokes that life can skim.
In this grand show, my thoughts are whim,
And laughter echoes when lights grow grim.

Flickering Lights in a Closed Room

In a room where thoughts flicker bright,
I chase the echoes in delight.
With every spark, I've lost the fight,
To pin down wisdom that takes flight.

Shadows dance on walls of gray,
I ponder hard, then lose my way.
Each thought's a game I cannot play,
In this closed zone of light ballet.

The ceiling cracks tell tales untold,
Of moments missed and laughter bold.
I scratch my head, the thoughts grow cold,
Yet humor shines, a treasure gold.

So with each laugh, I shut the door,
To keep the chaos I adore.
In flickering lights, I seek for more,
A funny tome of life's rapport.

Inkling of Wisdom in Innocent Laughter.

In moments bright, we chase the jest,
A giggle here, a sly little quest.
What's wisdom worth if lost in mirth?
We ponder more with jokes than birth.

A tiny thought, like cotton candy,
Dissolves too quick, isn't that dandy?
Life's a riddle wrapped in a pun,
The answer's clear, yet hardly begun.

Faces aglow, we laugh till it hurts,
While juggling snacks and silly shirts.
In the chaos, we find our way,
Forget the rest, let's laugh today!

So grab a friend, and share a grin,
The world's a game, come on, let's win.
With all our laughs, the truth can shine,
Life's not so bad, I think we're fine!

Whispers of Forgotten Dreams

Chasing shadows in the evening light,
Whispers tease, fading out of sight.
Dreams like bubbles, they rise and pop,
Then giggles spill, they never stop.

A paper boat on a puddle bright,
Floating by with laughter, what a sight!
We planned a grand quest to find the spice,
But ended up with pizza—oh, how nice!

With every sigh and every snort,
We search for wisdom in a comic sort.
The dreams we chase, they slip and slide,
Yet through the laughs, there's joy inside.

So hold your dreams with softened hands,
Let whispers lead to wacky plans.
For life's a chuckle, it's plain to see,
Forget the rules, let laughter be free!

Ephemeral Echoes of Existence

In fleeting time, we dart and dash,
Echoes ring, then go with a splash.
Thoughts like confetti, they swirl and fly,
Only to vanish like clouds in the sky.

With every sneeze, we change our course,
A joke about socks—a comedic force.
We laugh so hard, we can hardly breathe,
In the fleeting moments, joy takes its leave.

Eggs on the counter, we're crafting fun,
A breakfast debate, who said we shun?
The answers flee on joke-laden air,
Lost amid laughter, do we even care?

So treasure the giggles, and don't forget,
In chaos of life, there's little regret.
For in the echoes, we find our place,
With laughs that linger and smiles that lace.

When Clarity Slips Away

A moment of thought, then poof it's gone,
Like finding the cat at the break of dawn.
The brain is fuzzy; where's that neat spark?
We chuckle and groan in the middle of the dark.

Searching for answers, we trip on our words,
A tangle of tongue like jumbled birds.
Yet laughter bubbles in the midst of plight,
We dance to confusion, embracing the night.

Jokes like pillows, so soft and round,
In absurdity, clarity's never found.
We stumble through moments, a comical spree,
And when we forget, we're still oh-so free!

So let's hold close that silly, wild haze,
With laughter and joy that endlessly plays.
For when clarity slips, let's just sway and grin,
Life's a grand stage; let the fun begin!

The Silence Between Heartbeats

In the pause where thoughts collide,
I lose track, my mind's a ride.
With every tick, my plans run late,
But laughing hard feels like fate.

Searching for that missing clue,
I trip on laughter, how 'bout you?
The universe rolls its eyes, it's true,
While I just snack on cosmic goo.

A puzzle piece lost in time,
I hum a tune, forget the rhyme.
In chaos, I find my spark,
And dance around in the dark.

So here we are, a charming mess,
Enjoying life in all its excess.
Forget the answers, let's just play,
With silly hats, we'll seize the day.

Signs Written in Soft Footsteps

In gentle steps upon the ground,
I hear whispers that spin around.
They say to laugh, don't take a stand,
Just twirl about, hand in hand.

Each footprint tells a different tale,
Of ice cream dreams and ships that sail.
Stumbling on the path to bliss,
I shrug and blow a playful kiss.

Lost in thought, I see a sign,
But hey, wait, that's just a vine!
I chuckle low, it's all a game,
Tomorrow's just a silly name.

So here we go, on this wild spree,
With giggles shared from me to thee.
In laughter's arms, we shall remain,
And step in sync like falling rain.

Deconstructing the Fabric of a Dream

I caught a dream, or so I swear,
It danced around without a care.
With threads so bright, but where's the seam?
I laughed and lost the crafty scheme.

Each stitch I pulled unraveled fun,
A patchwork quilt that's never done.
In crazy colors, life unfurled,
A riddle wrapped in a twirled world.

A button popped, it spun and flew,
And landed on some purple goo.
It giggled back, what a fine sight!
Just chaos wrapped in cozy light.

So let's create with silly grace,
Forget the rules, we'll set the pace.
In whirling threads, we find our theme,
Enjoying all the wacky dream.

Wistful Glances at Forgotten Tomorrows

A glance ahead, a smile so shy,
I wave at dreams that flutter by.
Tomorrow's plans? Oh, what a bluff!
They slip away, but laughs are tough.

I scribble notes on paper planes,
And watch them soar through life's refrains.
With every flap, they giggle loud,
No worries here, I'm flying proud.

Between the dreams and silly sighs,
I find the fun in all the pies.
Whipped cream on a bursting joy,
Life's playful tricks, a gleeful ploy.

So let's embrace the whimsy's call,
In dance and laughter, let's enthrall.
For every tomorrow I forget,
Holds glimmers that I won't regret.

Dreams That Slipped Between Our Fingers

We chased our dreams like wild balloons,
But they popped with laughter, oh what a tune!
In the net of thoughts, we cast and threw,
Yet they danced away, as dreams often do.

Thoughts of grand plans on a Tuesday morn,
Yet by noon, all those visions were torn.
We held on tight, but they fell through the cracks,
Like slippery fish in a sea of comebacks.

Wandering Souls in the Realm of Now

We drift through life like aimless fish,
Fry in the pan of a whimsical wish.
With a wink and a nod, we missed the bus,
Then laughed at ourselves, now what's the fuss?

Lost in time, like socks in the wash,
Searching for answers in a jumbled posh.
So we sit back and chuckle a bit,
Who knew wandering was such a neat fit?

Elusive Clarity in a Hazy Daydream

I thought I found wisdom in a toast,
But the truth escaped like a polite ghost.
With a grin and a shrug, I pondered away,
Lost in the fog of a bright sunlit day.

A clear thought danced just out of reach,
It giggled and hid, a clever breach.
I waved at the clouds, hoping they'd hear,
But they just floated on, without any fear.

The Poetry of Unsaid Goodbyes

With goodbyes unspoken, we played a game,
Using smiles and winks, but none were the same.
We laughed through the tears, oh what a scene,
In the theater of life, where we all convene.

The words that we left unsaid took a bow,
Like clowns in a circus, we wonder how.
Yet in this jest, there's a sparkle of grace,
For in the chaos, we find our place.

A Melancholic Dance with Possibilities

Life's a jigsaw, pieces lost,
Searching corners, what was cost?
Weights of whims, they toss and turn,
In between, the lessons burn.

Waltz with doubts, a silly twirl,
Forget your keys? Oh, give a whirl!
Plans made clear, yet paths unwind,
Just try to dance, don't lose your mind.

Echoes of laughter, shadowed sighs,
In a whirlwind of endless tries.
A slip on dreams, a leap of faith,
Oh, what's the point? Is it just wraith?

So here we spin, round and round,
With giggles lost, yet joy is found.
A whimsied step, we laugh and cheer,
Life's a riddle, never clear.

Tides of Memory's Gentle Pull

Waves of thought crash on the shore,
Remembering what life holds in store.
A beach ball bounces, then rolls away,
Is the joke on us? Come what may.

Drifting on dreams, caught in the swell,
Did I leave the oven on? Oh well.
Sandy footprints in shifting grains,
We chase the tide, ignoring the pains.

Seagulls squawk their raucous song,
"Where'd you put that thing? Where's it gone?"
Salty winds whisper of bygone days,
Yet here we laugh in absurd, silly ways.

Catch the breeze, let worries drop,
With a belly laugh, we all can hop.
Amongst the waves, let's share our glee,
Forget the past; just let it be.

The Unseen Threads of Connection

A tangled web of tales we weave,
Each little moment, hard to believe.
How did I end up with this crew?
Guess life's a puzzle, is it not you?

It's a chat with friends over spilled tea,
And pondering life's great mystery.
Did I text my mom or was it my cat?
Connections twist, like a worn-out mat.

Each hello's a thread, some fray, some bind,
In the fabric of time, we humorously unwind.
Lost in the chatter, we circle the chat,
"Did I lend you money? Or was that a hat?"

With laughter ringing, we often forget,
Who needs a map? We're fine with a bet.
In the end, this tight-knit crew,
Keeps the mystery fun, with a cheerful view.

Flights of Fancy and Hidden Snags

Let's soar through clouds on wishes fine,
With dreams as wacky as old green brine.
Dare to hop, and then we glide,
But watch for turbulence on this ride!

Oh, to chase the stars with glee,
Yet trip on shoelaces, oh silly me!
Up we go, with visions grand,
Coming back down, 'twas never planned.

Paper planes and all that stuff,
Who said dreaming would be tough?
The sky's the limit, at least we hope,
But landing's tricky, oh boy, let's cope!

So let's embrace this playful fling,
Each wild idea that makes us sing.
For in the chaos, joy can snag,
It's fun to soar, but wear a flag!

Fleeting Thought of Eternal Now

A thought just flew right past my ear,
It whispered things I'd rather not hear.
Like socks that vanish in the dryer,
Or why my coffee's never dire.

I ponder deep and scratch my chin,
Then lose it all to where we've been.
Eternal youth or so they say,
I forgot where I put my way.

A twinkling star laughs in the night,
It's here, it's gone, a fleeting light.
I chase my thoughts like running hands,
While laughter slips through trembling strands.

Oh look, a cat with fishy dreams,
Lost in his world of sunny beams.
Let's toast to chaos, wild and free,
Even if it's all a hazy spree.

Laughter Echoing Through Empty Spaces

In empty rooms where echoes play,
A little chuckle fades away.
The walls might sigh, the ceiling creaks,
But laughter lingers, so unique.

A ticklish thought, a giggle flows,
Like sneaky whispers that no one knows.
I slipped on wisdom, fell on my face,
Oh well, I guess it's just our place.

Why ponder deep when jokes abound?
Life's a riddle, tightly wound.
Yet in its fibers, laughter spins,
With every twist, a chance to grin.

I found a smile beneath my shoe,
It asked for dance; should I pursue?
In empty spaces filled with glee,
The echoes bounce, and so do we.

Fragments of What Used to Be

I found a notebook on the floor,
It held my dreams from days of yore.
But most of it was scribbled jokes,
About the world and silly folks.

A pie chart drawn with crayons bright,
Sliced up the happiness in bite.
What did I love? I can't recall,
But I remember laughing—was that all?

So here I sit, with noodle mind,
Searching for gems that I can't find.
Fragments of moments float and tease,
Like socks that dance in playful breeze.

I'll raise a toast to lost pursuits,
To fragments piled like old worn boots.
In chaos, wisdom's often shrouded,
Yet in laughter, all is crowded.

In Search of an Elusive Truth

I chased a truth down winding roads,
With a map that flipped and heaved load.
Yet every sign just pointed back,
To questions cloaked in laughter's slack.

An answer hid beneath a chair,
She winked at me and tossed her hair.
I laughed so hard, I lost my shoe,
The truth proclaimed, 'I'm hiding too!'

Through garden paths and cloudy skies,
I searched for sense wrapped in disguise.
Yet in the winks and playful shouts,
I found that joy is what it's about.

So here's to truths that come and go,
Wrapped in laughter, all aglow.
In the pursuit of what we seek,
Let humor dance, and life unique!

Reflections in Every Surface We Forget

In a mirror, my face looks back,
But I can't recall the name of that snack.
Life's like a circus, all clowns and no glee,
I laugh 'cause it's silly, just look at me!

My phone buzzes loud, a message to scan,
What was it again? Oh, was it the plan?
I doodle in margins, my mind starts to drift,
Like the sock in the wash that just vanished, a gift.

Chasing my shadow, I stumble and trip,
What was I doing? Oh, give me a skip.
Lost in the nonsense, a joke I can't crack,
I think of a punchline, but it just won't pack.

Amidst all the chaos, I try to recall,
Was it lunch or a party? Or just nothing at all?
A giggle escapes as I fumble my way,
In this game of forget, I just want to play!

Shadows that Shroud Our Longing Hearts

In the shadow of night, what's that I yearn?
A slice of pizza? Oh, when will I learn?
Thoughts flit like moths, around the same light,
Does anyone know what's for dinner tonight?

Wander through memories, a confusing maze,
Was it you or the cat that caused this craze?
Chasing the shadows, I trip on my feet,
And laugh at the echoes, so silly and sweet.

A dream on the couch turns into a sneeze,
Why do I laugh when I feel ill at ease?
Was it yesterday's plight or tomorrow's delight?
Who knows what awaits in this whimsical flight?

Forgetful and fuzzy, I dance with the stars,
Collecting the laughter wrapped high in my jars.
Smiles slip away while I ponder alone,
In this echoing chamber, I'm finally home.

Fractals of Thoughts Never Expressed

Ideas spin round like a top on the floor,
What was I saying? Oh, what was the score?
Fractals of nonsense, a chaotic delight,
As I juggle my thoughts, they take off in flight.

I scribble some words, but they fade into mist,
Were they clever or dandy? I seem to have missed.
Each thought's a puzzle, all jumbled and mixed,
Like socks with their mates—it's an odd little fix.

Tangled in laughter, I weave through the mess,
Life's a grand riddle dressed up in a dress.
Join the parade of the lost and the found,
Where reason retreats and the giggles resound.

In this fractal dance, I embrace the absurd,
For the laughter we share speaks louder than words.
Let's sip on the nonsense, like lemonade sweet,
In this carnival of thoughts, we never compete!

Once Upon a Time We Almost Remembered

Once upon a time, we dreamed this great quest,
But what was the goal? Oh, I must have missed.
In a story so tangled, I can't find the plot,
Did someone just say that? Or was it a thought?

We gathered with friends, all whimsical glee,
What were we laughing about? Wait, was it me?
Pages of life turn, but the words slip away,
I'm pretty sure we're winning at least—hey, hooray!

The clock strikes a tune, or was that just snores?
In this fairy tale, we unlock all the doors.
Magic residues dust on our shoes,
But wait—who's the hero? I get so confused!

With wands made of laughter, we write our own fate,
In this fable of mischief, we navigate late.
As the chorus of giggles rings bright in the air,
Once upon a time, we were always somewhere!

www.ingramcontent.com/pod-product-compliance
Lightning Source LLC
Chambersburg PA
CBHW071830160426
43209CB00003B/261